_____

Copyright © 2017 by Ophelia S. Lewis
All rights reserved. No part of this publication may be reproduced, distributed or transmitted in any form or by any means, without prior written permission.

This is a work of fiction. Names, characters, places, and incidents are a product of the author's imagination.

Village Tales Publishing
www.villagetalespublishing.com
www.oass.villagetalespublishing.com
www.villagetalespublishing.com/childrensbooks

Book Cover by OASS

ISBN 9781945408144
eISBN 9781945408151
LCCN 2017908156

Printed in the USA

Toby Pannoh's Good Manners for Boys and Girls

Written by Ophelia S. Lewis

Illustrations by
Shabamukama Osbert

Dedicated to Liyah Matthews

Toby's family portray

No matter where you live, and no matter what your age, good boys and girls must have good manners to be polite. This is what my parents and grandparents have taught me, my older brother, Dorbor, and my older sister, Felo. My name is, Toby Pannoh. I am eight years old and in the third grade.

My family lives in Barclayville, Grand Kru County, Liberia. I live with my parents and siblings in a big brick house. My father's name is, Borbor Pannoh. He is a police officer. My mother, Nyema Pannoh, is a school teacher. Everybody calls her, Mrs. Pannoh. She teaches the fifth and sixth graders at our school.

I have two sisters, Felo, who is twelve years old and Mah, my baby sister, is only five. My brother, Dorbor, is sixteen and has a lot of friends. I like to watch Dorbor and his friends play ball.

Grandma Jloh Pannoh and Grandpa Siakah Pannoh live only half a mile away. They are always visiting us. My other grandparents,

Grandma Gen Nyon and Grandpa Tor Nyon, live many miles away. They live in Monrovia, where I spend my vacation when school closes.

I wanted my little sister, Mah, to learn good manners too. So to teach her, I arranged some rules of good manners that I have learned with the alphabets. Mah is in kindergarten. She does not know how to read on her own, but she listens and she talks. I know that she will have fun learning the rules of good behavior using the alphabets. This would be a good way for her to practice reciting them.

Each letter of the alphabet is used in teaching common standards with the ideas of the right conduct and good character. Grandpa Siakah says that good manners are politeness and courtesy, which stand for thoughtful and kind consideration for others.

Boys and girls can always practice respectful habits at home, at school, and when they are out with the family. And especially, while playing with other boys and girls. They can even be polite while sitting at the table during dinner time.

Mah may be only five years old, but good manners can be taught as soon as your little brother or sister can understand what you are saying. Some little brothers and sisters can even learn good manners at just three years old. How cool is that!

Did I not tell you that Grandpa Siakah is a pastor? He is the pastor at our church. One of the things he taught our family is the Golden Rule;

Always treat others the way you would want them to treat you.

Since my mother is a school teacher, I will start with the first letter of the alphabet.

A a

Arrive On Time. Try to always be on time, even if your mother is not your teacher. It is good to be neat, and have clean hands too.

B b

Grandma Jloh is a market woman. She works in the marketplace near our house. Sometimes after work, Grandma Jloh brings me and Mah a fruit or a toy. Mah can hardly wait to get what she has brought us, and she cries. Then Grandma Jloh tells her to Be Patient. When someone asks you to wait, be patient. Wait.

C c

I always see Papa open the car door for Mama to get in, and then he gets in. So I hold doors open for others, especially when our grandparents come to visit. If you are walking ahead of someone, hold the door open for them when you reach it first. Remember to Close Doors Quietly, too.

Mah loves the sound of a door-slam, be it a car or a room door. Be careful with door-slams. Your baby brother or baby sister could get hurt if their little finger gets caught in a door-slam.

D d

The letter D is a tough one. Sometimes I pout, and Mama tells me, "Toby, Don't Pout. It makes your handsome face look ugly."

Sometimes it is hard not to show how unhappy you are. At times I mope around and pout, especially when Mama asks me to do something while I'm playing with my toys. It's better to be a good example for your little sister, or little brother, to follow. So don't pout, even when you are mad.

E e

Grandpa Siakah reminds me to keep my elbows off counters and tables. I don't know why you should keep your elbows off the table while you eat, but it is considered rude to keep your elbows on the table. If it is your culture, or not, it is considered impolite when you do. So to be polite and considerate of other people's comfort, keep your Elbows off tables, please.

F f

One time Mah lost her favorite toy, and the whole family had to look for it. Felo found the toy underneath Mah's bed and gave it back to her. Everyone was happy to see Mah laughing again. When you find something that belongs to another person, it is good to return it. Owning it means you could be stealing it.

That's because Finders can't always be keepers.

G g

Mah hates to take naps. She cries every time Mama puts her down to nap. When I am having fun, I hate to go to bed early. But once I do, I get enough rest to start a new day. Go to bed on time without fussing. You will not be tired at school, or church, the next day.

H h

I like Dorbor because he is a good big brother. He loves to play catch with me sometimes after school. Because I am much smaller than his friends, I watch him play football with them rather than join in. When the ball goes out of bound, me and my friends race to get it, then throw it back into play. But throwing most things might get friends hurt. It is better to Hand things over. Sometimes I hand over the Bible to Dorbor and ask him to read me a story.

I i

When a new idea comes in my head, I get excited and want to share it right away. But while someone else is doing something, or speaking, it is rude to cut in. Here's a really good advice, Interrupting is not nice.

J j

Sure, jokes can make people feel good. A loud laugh is a blast for practical jokes. Chuckles are even good for some bloopers. But **Jokes should never hurt others.** It is never okay to make fun of someone that is different from you.

K k

Every time I come to a closed door, I always knock. Before entering a room, it is often courteous to knock at the door when it is tightly closed; knock even when it is slightly opened. Knock and wait to hear, "Come In;" then open the door. Do not forget to close the door quietly.

L l

Be attentive while someone is talking. When you are in school or church, Listen Closely to hear what the speaker says. You will hear the message and understand. Be a good listener in class.

M m

When I want something from the fruit basket, I always ask by saying, "Grandma, may I have an orange, please?"

After you've asked, don't insist on getting what you've asked for right away. Give them time. "May I," is a good way to ask. You just have to ask once, and wait for a reply.

N n

This is a rule for men and boys. Gentlemen, big and small. It is poor manners to wear a hat while sitting at a table eating. Before the family sits to eat our dinner, Papa says to me and Dorbor, "No hat at the table, please."

While Papa and the boys take off their hats, Mama does not put her purse or handbag on the table. She puts it on the small table that we are not using.

O o

Grandpa Siakah says rules are DOs and DON'Ts to follow. Rules are made to keep everyone safe. When at home, or at school, when you are walking or playing; follow the clues and Obey the Rules.

P p

These three actions are very important. Stop. Look. Listen. Each of these action gets you ready for what to expect, and what you do not expect. To be safe, Pay Attention all the time.

Q q

Grandpa Siakah says there is a time for everything. There's a time to talk and a time to be Quiet when everyone is. Here is a list of places where you need to be quiet; at school, at the hospital, at church, at the mosque, the library, at a funeral, at the cinema and at the museum. We try to be quiet when watching TV with the family.

R r

It is never OK to be rude to anyone. My brother, Dorbor, is my role model. I copy his behavior and do my best when I compete. I do not bully or cheat in the games. If you win and others lose, bragging is not courteous. I want to be a Role Model like Dorbor, by being kind to others. I am a role model to Mah, like Dorbor is a role model to me.

S s

Although I share my toys with Mah, she has not learned to share with others. It is not good to be selfish. Sharing your toys, or treats, is a good way to make friends. Sharing makes others happy.

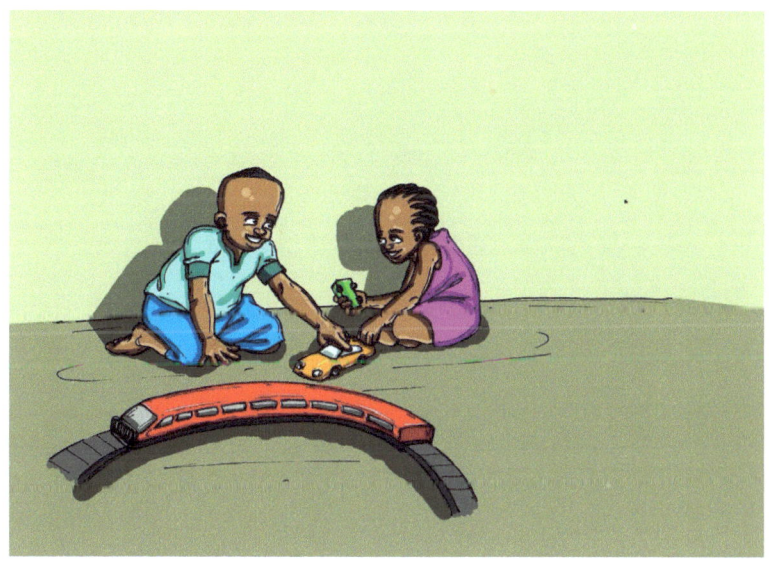

T t

Always say, "Thank You" and "Please" to be respectful. These are good courtesies. And then when someone says to you, "Thank you," you can say, "You are welcome."

U u

Neither should children, nor adults, swear, cuss, or use bad language, whether we are at home or out. Polite expressions, or a pat on the back, makes people happy. Use positive words to give others compliments.

V v

Different families do things their special way; be it religion, culture or race. Your views of others must be respectful. It is always good to learn about what makes other people different. Then, respect and accept their differences. Don't forget, you are different to them. Views of others must be handled tenderly.

W w

Grandpa Siakah says it is always good to help others when you can. Help yourself, and look out for friends and playmates too. Be patient, and try not to jump ahead. To wait your turn means you are the next person to do, or get, something. Calmly, Wait your turn.

Burps and farts are hard to control when you are a little boy or girl. You won't be able to hold in the noise until you are at least eight years old, like me. Mama says it is just our little body letting out air. But, it is not polite to make such noises in public.

When you burp, or if you fart, or if someone is standing in your way; when you want to join a conversation, or if you want someone's attention; "eXcuse me, please," is a key phrase.

Excuse does not start with the letter X. I don't know a good manner word that does. So I am using the X in excuse. Isn't that smart? Mama says it is.

Y y

When Mama calls me, I answer her by saying, "Yes, Mama." It sounds better than saying, "yep" or "yeah" or "uh-huh" or "Yup".

Answer nicely when you are called, "Yes" sounds better than "Yeah" or "Yup".

Z z

All boys and girls like to play. The happiest time is during the day while we are playing. Playtime is fun time. We jump. We chase each other in tag. We climb up, then hurriedly climb down.

We, boys and girls, must try to remember not to run or jump around in the house or in the classroom. Zooming is meant for outdoors!

I am proud of Mah. Now that she knows good manners and her alphabets, Mah will join Team Sapo and get this certificate. After Mama signs it, Papa will put it in a frame and hang it on the wall in the living room. Everybody will see it. I bet next time when Grandma Gen and Grandpa Tor visit, they will be proud too.

You can get this certificate too. Just learn good manners using the alphabets. Sapo would be happy you did.

Ms. Ophelia S. Lewis **Author**

A descendant of Liberia settlers and a Gbande chief, Ophelia S. Lewis has written several books that exhibit Liberia and provide views into Liberia society one cannot get from the headlines. Author of the popular heart-man novels, (*Heart Men* and *Dead Gods* (HM2)—Ms. Lewis has also written two collections of short stories, *The Dowry of Virgins & Other Stories* and *Montserrado Stories*; a book of essays, *My Dear Liberia*; and a collection of poems, *Journeys*. She has written several children's books; *A is for Africa*, *The Good Manner Alphabets* (How to be a super polite kid), *I'm About To*, and *Where in the World is Liberia* (puzzles gamebook).

Ms. Lewis writes full-time and lives with her family in Georgia. Connect with her; read her blog, BeEncouraged, send a friend request on Facebook (www.facebook.com/ophelia.lewis), follow her on twitter @ophie2020, or visit her personal website for updates on her latest work, www.ophelialewis.com.

Mr. Shabamukama Osbert **Illustrator**

Shabamukama Osbert was born on July 7, 1990 in the small village of Mbonwa, Ibanda District, Western Uganda. Since his mother died when he was five-years-old, Osbert was raised by a single father in a big family with eleven other siblings. Art has always been a passion, even during his primary and secondary education. In 2016, he earned his bachelor's degree in industrial and fine art from Makerere University.

Mr. Osbert is a painter, structural designer and an illustrator. He loves art. During his free time, he enjoys photography, travelling, painting and doing illustrations. Mr. Osbert currently lives in Kampala, Uganda.

Connect with Mr. Osbert on Facebook, @Ashaba Osbert.

Other Sapo Children's Books you will love...

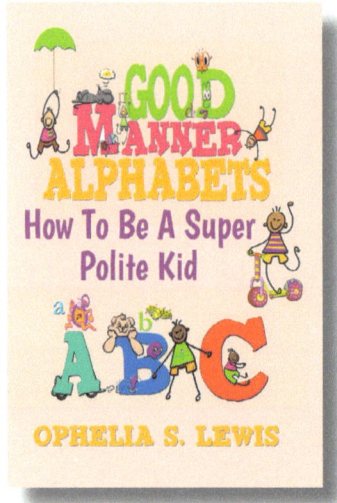

Trim Size: 8" x 5"
5-Pack High quality glossy printed certificate

OR

Get this beautiful High Quality Glossy Print certificate with each copy purchased off Village Tales Publishing web site.

**Good Manner Alphabets
(how to be a polite kid)**
By Ophelia S. Lewis

ISBN: 9780985362515
eISBN: 9780985362553
Ages 3 & Up | Grade Level: Pre-K to Kindergarten
Publication Date: November , 2014
Page Count: 36 | 8 x 10 | Paperback
Publisher: Village Tales Publishing

Ballah Makes Shapes
By Augustus Y. Voah
ISBN: 9781945408199
eISBN: 978-1945408205
Ages 6 years & Up | Grade One
Publication Date: July 2017
Page Count:42 | 6 x 9 | Paperback
Publisher: Village Tales Publishing

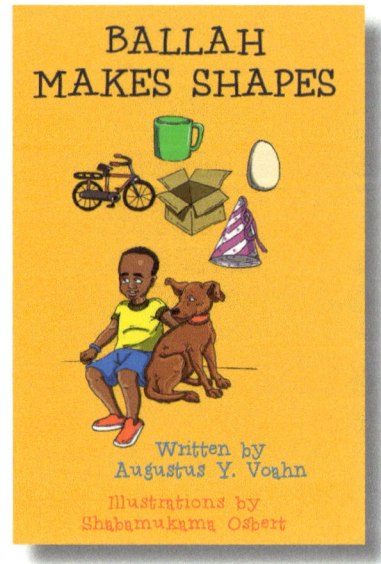

Uncle Jallah Will Fix It
By Augustus Y. Voahn

ISBN: 9781945408120
eISBN: 978-1945408137
Ages 6-12 years old
Grade Level: 3-7
Publication Date: April , 2017
Page Count: 36 | 8 x 10 | Paperback
Publisher: Village Tales Publishing

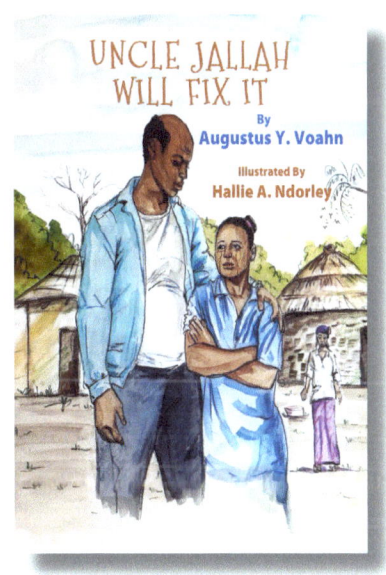

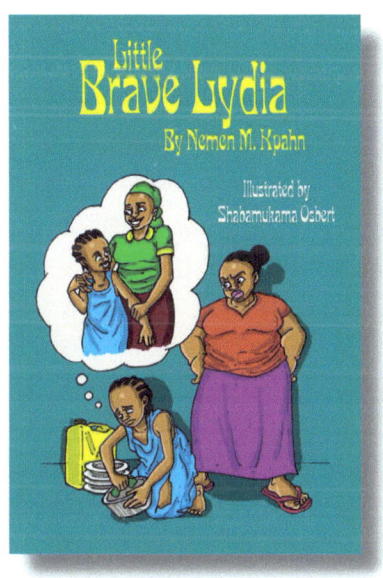

Village Tales Publishing is a proud member of the Liberia Literary Society

Little Brave Lydia
By Nemen M. Kpahn

ISBN: 9781945408120
eISBN: 978-1945408137
Ages 6-12 years old | Grade Level: 3-7
Publication Date: April , 2017
Page Count: 60 | 6 x 9 | Paperback
Publisher: Village Tales Publishing

All books can be purchased on our website at
www.villagetalespublishing.com

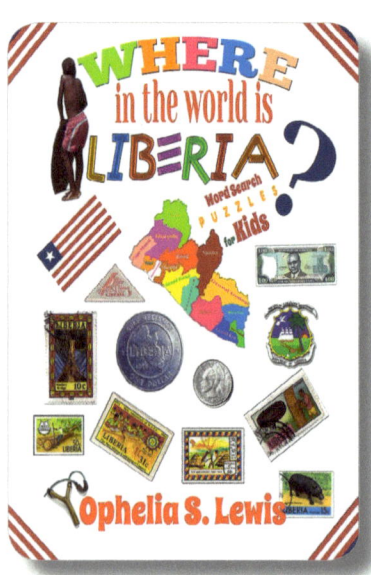

Where in the World is Liberia
By Ophelia S. Lewis

Age Range: 6-12 years old
Grade Level: 2-7
Pub. Date: March 18, 2016
ISBN: 9780985362577
Page Count: 60 | 8.5 x 11
Paperback
Children's Books-Education
Activities-Games-Puzzle
Publisher: Village Tales Publishing

I'm About To
By Ophelia S. Lewis

ISBN: 9781945408120
eISBN: 978-1945408137
Ages 6-12 years old
Grade Level: 3-7
Publication Date: April , 2017
Page Count: 36 | 8 x 10
Paperback
Publisher: Village Tales Publishing

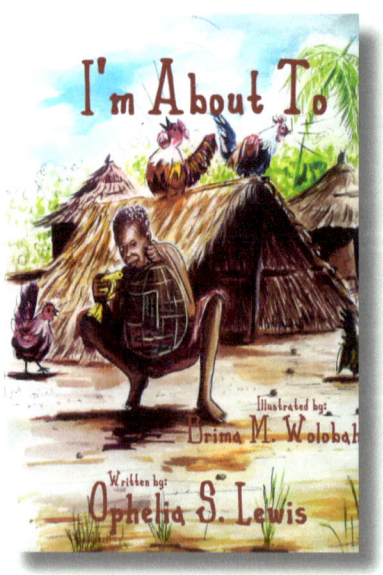

Available at all online and retail bookstores, Paperback and eBook at Amazon.com

Enchanting Voices anthology was written by the winners and finalists of the 1st Annual Sexy Like A Book Poetry Competition for Liberian Girls, Lisa Harris, Victoria Daye, Faith Gray, Marshad Beyslow, Maxita George and Odell Garkpah; and edited by founder, Ms. Patrice Juah; published by Village Tales Publishing.

Interested in supporting the initiative? Visit their website at www.sexylikeabook.com and buy the book. 100% of the proceeds from this book will go towards scaling up efforts and providing scholarships and educational resources to Liberian girls, particularly those in rural communities.

@sexylikeabook

learning with Sapo

Our world is filled with amazing people, places, and things; why not publish books that will help teachers and parents include **our** world into **our** children's reading practice?

Sapo Children's Book are academic and reading books students can relate to culturally.

~Reading Our World~

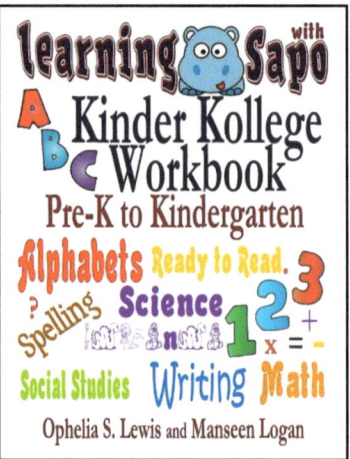

ISBN-13: 9781945408168
Format: Paperback | 8.5 x 11
Pages: 100

Every child has the ability to change the world; we want to make sure they can. African children are still struggling to catch up to the rest of the world in the age of digital transformation. Three-to-six-year-olds are enthusiastic learners, and in order to explore their desire to understand things and build a solid learning foundation, quality scholastic education is required. **Learning With Sapo** is an initiative emphasized on the academic development of young children by making available books and workbooks that help parents and teachers inspire literacy and learning for children in Africa. Learning With Sapo is focus on publishing academic books students can relate to culturally. Liberia Literary Society partners with **Sapo's Children's Book** (Village Tales Publishing children's division) to do just that.

Please support this needed cause by making a donation at **www.liberialiterarysociety.org** website.

Visit our websites for updates
www.schoolonthego.liberialiterarysociety.org
www.liberialiterarysociety.org

If we can inspire a child to love education at a very young age, then we are doing something about possible child labor prevention. Strenuous work keeps children between the ages of seven and fifteen out of school. Poverty might be a major reason, however, traditional beliefs plays a part. Being 'hardworking' seem a positive goal set for young boys and girls, rather than education. At times, most people don't even recognize the rights of children, other's or their own. Liberia Literary Society believes there is a good chance to combat and change this mindset (harmful practice) through our initiative, School-On-The-Go.

School-on-the-Go is a program designed to teach young children who are out of school, and at the marketplace with their mothers. This provides pre-K, kindergarten and first grade scholastic education at the Marketplace. These children are offered backpacks with writing supplies, reading books, workbooks, and other school-supply items used by kindergartners everywhere, and will be used as a teaching tool. Using a one-on-one approach, as opposed to a classroom setting, this program will prepare students with a solid educational foundation, making a difference in the lives of children as they prepare for their educational journey. No child should be left behind. Besides providing quality scholastic education, this also create jobs for high school seniors (part-time), college students (part-time) and (full-time) teachers. One teacher (to 5 students) will be hired to conduct one-hour tutoring session per child, using the Kinder Kollege workbook and a Kindle reader for kids.

You can support this needed cause by making a donation with cash or school supplies. Please visit our sponsor website at: www.liberialiterarysociety.org.

www.ingramcontent.com/pod-product-compliance
Lightning Source LLC
Chambersburg PA
CBHW041755040426
42446CB00001B/47